SYSTEMS OF DEFENSE

SYSTEMS OF DEFENSE

A Structural Composition of Defense Mechanisms

by J. A. Gucci

SYSTEMS OF DEFENSE
A Structural Composition of Defense Mechanisms
by J. A. Gucci Copyright © 2026 J. A. Gucci

First Edition

ISBN: 978-1-972788-12-7

Printed in the United States of America

www.jagucci.com

CONTENTS

Pressure Systems

Transformations

Withdrawal & Reaction

Identity & Relation

Redistribution

Transfer & Separation

PREFACE

These poems operate under Absolute Composition.

No thresholds are provided. No transitions are supplied. No internal states are explained. What appears is structure in partial form.

The reader is not positioned as interpreter, but as participant. Completion does not occur within the text. It occurs through reconstruction.

Each poem presents a condition without resolution. Movement must be inferred. Relation must be established. The systems are not described. They are enacted.

As in clinical observation, structure is derived from surface. The poems do not explain defense mechanisms. They require their assembly.

Meaning is not embedded. It is produced through engagement.

Failure to resolve is not an error of the text.

"Nothing is missing.
You are."

PRESSURE SYSTEMS

Projection

Cold white
boiling black

clouds,
crawling—

pale violet.

Repression

Solid smooth
cobalt blue,

cleave.

Sinking floating
iceberg.

Denial

Sun-scorched
shimmering heath

cold—
windless air

floating—
island in the sky.

Splitting

Barren brittle
balk,

rumbles—

liquid dust plumes.

Reaction Formation

Red moss carpet
green
glistening sundew

smiling—
bog body.

TRANSFORMATIONS

Conversion

Snap, jaw
tail

thrashing—

stump.

Undoing

Swollen date palms
nestled in silt,

wandering dune
creeping,
leaping—

shriveled date palms
buried in sand.

Rationalization

Warm air plumes
spiraling

putrid flesh rot
hooked—

brittle bones.

Intellectualization

Solid brittle
desert

deluge—

shrinking muddy chasm—
dusty hexagons.

WITHDRAWAL AND REACTION

Isolation of Affect

Muzzle wrinkle—

Joey
dropped—

dusty footprints.

Regression

Warm current
cold—

gelatinous lump
slumped on the ridge—

umbrella bell.

Acceptance

Stiff
swollen green
waxy sheen,

cracked matte
heath
glistening sticky

stem,
wilted.

IDENTITY AND RELATION

Identification

Scarlet king
skin
ringed yellow, red
nestled in loam

black
fluttering wings
dusty footprints.

Introjection

Worker

wrapped in jelly,
swallow—

Queen.

REDISTRIBUTION

Sublimation

Hot throat spewing
liquid rock,

black billowing
ash
alight on a hill—

whispering bells.

Altruism

Stylet and lancelet
rammed into hide—

twitching
still curl.

TRANSFER AND SEPARATION

Displacement

Flat
languid river
mound

crevasse splay,
rushing—

wet forest,
stagnant oxbow lakes.

Suppression

Downriver slabs
jammed—

plodding—
creak.

Compartmentalization

Glinting and glittering
waves
lapping waves,

gloop—

still bog bodies
rotting
egg air.

Idealization

Desert dust
sunk in a drop

drifting
frozen air—

snowflake.

Devaluation

Smooth
limestone slab,

rain
crazing stone

forest.

Dissociation

Pulsing green
flash,

moonrise—

scattered green
flashes.

COLOPHON

Systems of Defense: A Structural Composition of Defense Mechanisms was composed in 2026.

The text is set in a modern serif typeface.

All poems were written and arranged by J. A. Gucci.

The system continues.

www.ingramcontent.com/pod-product-compliance
Ingram Content Group UK Ltd.
Pitfield, Milton Keynes, MK11 3LW, UK
UKHW042011190726
13854UKWH00005B/2243

9 781972 788127